DEMONS OF ADDICTION

DEMONS OF ADDICTION

by: CHIP SLOAN

XULON PRESS

Xulon Press
2301 Lucien Way #415
Maitland, FL 32751
407.339.4217

www.xulonpress.com

Printed in the United States of America

Paperback ISBN-13: 978-1-6628-3947-4
Ebook ISBN-13: 978-1-6628-3948-1

This book is

dedicated to

The glory of God

David Andrew Sloan

May 28, 1972–October 1, 2018

His Chains Are Gone

He's Been Set Free

Hallelujah

Praise the Lord

Table of Contents

Demons of Addiction

This is the heartbreaking story of a young man whose life was shattered by substance abuse.

We buried our son on October 3, 2018. He was forty-six-years old. He should have been in the prime of his life, but due to thirty-six years of tobacco, alcohol, and drug abuse he was a very sick man. He suffered from MRSA (an infection that is extremely resistant to antibiotics), immune deficiency disorder, recurring pneumonia, hepatitis C, coronary artery disease, fibromyalgia, endocarditis, depression, and cirrhosis. In addition to these ailments, he was confined to a wheelchair due to a condition called drop foot, which manifested itself due to back surgery because of MRSA infection. He'd lost his teeth due to the abuse of meth and cocaine.

The last four years of his life were spent mostly in hospitals and halfway houses. From March 2015 to December 2017, he had 25 admittances (that I am aware of) for a total of 215 days. He was in ICU at The Medical University of South Carolina for two weeks for pneumonia and sepsis. I did not think he would survive, but he did. I applaud the doctors and nurses for the excellent care he received at MUSC.

He'd also had some unnecessary surgeries, including varicose veins, a broken finger sustained in a fight was operated on several times, and unnecessary tooth extractions, anything to get pain medication. He became a master at manipulating doctors and nurses and emergency room personnel. He would go from doctor to doctor to get pain medication. Sometimes he would have as many as five or six bottles of ninety pain pills each. This was enough to sell for $20 each on the street and enough to stay high for some time. Doctors willingly wrote these prescriptions and on occasion even encouraged him to have unnecessary surgeries. Sometimes doctors unknowingly exacerbate a situation.

In these hospitalizations and doctor visits he never paid a dime (to my knowledge). I suppose they just wrote his bills off as bad debt. The last two years of his life, he did manage to get full disability and a food card.

On several occasions, he'd enrolled at technical schools, not to get an education but to get money. He found that if you enrolled as a homeless, jobless, person, the government would give you cash money to go to school! He would get pay-outs of several thousand dollars twice per semester. He never attended class and would get a doctor's excuse and then get even more money. Unfortunately, most of the money went for drugs and was used up in a matter of days or weeks. My experience has shown me that our government is not set up to help addicts but to enable them. He was not "The Lone Ranger" here because he learned how to manipulate the educational system from other drug addicted friends. You don't have to be a rocket scientist to figure how much this one "humanitarian act" costs our government nationwide.

He lived in halfway houses and cheap, dirty motels when he had money, or on the street as a homeless person, when he had no money. This was a way of life for him, and he became accustomed to it and was content to live like this. Some of the halfway houses where he lived would have twenty homeless, addicted men in one small room. Others were not that crowded. There were times when he turned to begging on the street to get money to eat, but unfortunately most of the money would be spent on drugs. On one occasion, he lost thirty pounds in less than two weeks. When on a binge, very little if any food and water is consumed. This is very unhealthy and the reason so many addicts die.

Sometimes when things would get bad, he would check himself into one of the many drug rehab programs he knew about, none of which worked for him. He would do well for a time then leave of his own accord or get kicked out. Most of these programs are maintained by donations, some are church affiliated and require the client to work but other than that, they are free of charge and provide food, shelter, and clothing. These programs really try to help the addict and they do a remarkable job with the funds they have. They are good people doing a good deed for mankind.

All the government programs that I am aware of are staffed by professional people and, believe it or not, treat drug addiction with drugs. As a parent, or loved one, when you are desperate, you will reach out for any help that is available, anything that will give you a few days relief. I recall several times he was released from a government program with a prescription for the drug he was trying to stop using. How insane is that?

All these programs can work for the addict if the addict can admit that they have a problem and they truly want help. I believe that the only way for the addict to become sober and stay sober is by placing his/her trust in Jesus Christ. I have personally witnessed many teenagers, young adults, and median adults who try to get sober without trusting Jesus and they are unsuccessful at becoming or staying sober. Christ is the answer, the only answer.

Life History

A the age of twelve years, he made a choice to cut school with a friend. They went to the friend's house, got into his father's liquor cabinet and consumed enough alcohol to make them drunk. My son told me years later that he liked the taste and the way it made him feel. Basically, he was hooked after only one drink.

At the age of thirteen, his mother (we had divorced) had him placed in a mental hospital (without my knowledge and against my wishes). This turned out to be the first step toward a lifelong dependence on prescription drugs and doctors and counselors. I am not saying that this is a bad thing, but in our case the outcome was not a positive experience.

Upon the advice of a friend, we placed him in an adolescent drug program at the age of fourteen, in New York City. After two days, he was sent home for fighting. The next two years saw us just surviving, doing what we could to keep the boat afloat.

Later that year, his mother (again without my knowledge) placed him in STRAIGHT, an adolescent drug program in Atlanta, Georgia. He attended a local high school there where he made the honor roll and was an exemplary student and client of the program. After eighteen months he graduated STRAIGHT and was hired there as a counselor (something that rarely happened). After six months as a counselor there he informed us that he was leaving STRAIGHT and his job. Soon after leaving, he was using drugs again. We later found that he was hanging out with a group of his peers who also had graduated from STRAIGHT. They all had relapsed and were using drugs. This was a choice that he'd made. No one forced him to leave his job or begin using drugs again.

The next seventeen years saw his use of tobacco, alcohol, and illegal and prescription drugs escalate. Many drug rehab programs were tried only for him to quit or graduate and immediately return to abusing drugs. This happened because he made lots of "friends" at these rehab programs, with many of whom he kept in close contact. This "network" of friends always assured him that he could get drugs or a place to stay for a few days as the need arose.

We witnessed many encounters with the law, with numerous arrests, and many trips to emergency rooms. This became an insane way of life for him and for us. As he got deeper into drugs, our relationship with our son deteriorated to the point that there was no longer meaningful or reasonable conversation. We found ourselves always talking about his "drug problem" and desperately trying to talk him out of his insanity. Nothing we did or said changed his lifestyle. He even began selling drugs. Because he thought he was invincible, he began stealing from his supplier. He moved around quite a bit, and at one point he was almost beaten to death and executed by a drug dealer from whom he had stolen money and drugs. The protective hand of God was on him as a deputy sheriff just happened to be driving by on a lonely road in Virginia where the execution was taking place and the executioners fled the scene.

An automobile accident occurred when he and a druggie friend were driving to meet a drug dealer to purchase cocaine and were involved in a head-on collision that resulted in an innocent lady receiving massive injuries and his friend, who was driving under the influence, being killed instantly. My son got out with only a broken collar bone. Again, the protective hand of God was upon him.

Another automobile accident occurred when he was riding with four druggie friends. They hit a natural gas meter that caused quite an explosion. One girl in the car received a broken back and several other passengers were slightly injured. As before, he was not injured at all. The irony here was that a lawyer who was listening to a police band radio arrived on the scene and each passenger got a $20,000 settlement because the gas meter did not have protective poles around it.

My son was an excellent chef and held prestigious positions at many country clubs and restaurants. He never was employed longer than several months at any one job because he would report to work high or simply would not report at all. This became the norm until he became too sick to work and received disability.

Helping or Enabling?

L iving with an addict causes a person or family to sec-
ond-guess themselves almost daily. You want to help the
addict without enabling them. The problem here is that there
is such a fine line between helping and enabling that you never
know if you are making the right decision. The addict seems to
always be in the driver's seat of the dysfunctional family car. It
seems that they are always calling the shots and putting other
family members in jeopardy. Anyone who is living with an
addict is constantly placed in the most stressful of situations.

I have listed below a few of the situations we were placed in:

Many times, I would get a call from my son to come and
help him move. I would hook up my trailer and go where he
was living and help him move what bit of furniture and belong-
ings he had to his new residence. Sometimes this would be a
three-to-four-hour drive one-way. I would always agree to help,
knowing in my heart that I was enabling, but I did it anyway.
My helping him move never once helped him to become sober.
I was an enabler, and I was sicker than he was.

He usually had a small motorcycle or scooter as his means
of transportation. During the winter months his stepmother
and I would buy him insulated coveralls, gloves, and other
winter gear only to find that he would sell them to buy drugs.
I repeated this action many times when he would tell me that

they were stolen. I knew better, but I didn't want him to be cold. I was an enabler, and I was sicker than he was.

My son and I loved to fish. I had a small aluminum boat and motor that I decided to give him hoping it would help him to fish more and use drugs less. He sold it in less than 24 hours. My thinking was insane, and I was an enabler and much sicker than my son.

Many times, he would ask for money because his money had been stolen, or someone had taken advantage of him. Most times I felt sorry for him that he was broke and after a lengthy useless lecture I would give him the money. He was always going to pay me back, but payback day never came. I was an enabler, and I was sicker than he was.

The holidays and the addict's birthday are a most difficult times of the year. We might not hear from him for weeks but close to the holidays he would begin calling. He would always show up at Christmas and on his birthday and we would always have lots of presents for him because he didn't have anything because he'd spent his money on drugs. Buying him presents never helped him to become sober. In fact, it only served to worsen his addiction, because he would sell his gifts or trade them for drugs. We bought him presents and we were enabling him, and we were sicker than he was.

When he was in STRAIGHT, his stepmother and I drove four hours to Atlanta every Monday afternoon to attend mandatory meetings. We also had assigned weekends when we would rent a hotel room and spend the weekend with him and other young men in the program. Needless to say, STRAIGHT was not an inexpensive venture. It was very taxing on us because we both were assistant principals in middle schools. When he graduated

STRAIGHT, we bought him a car, in less than six months he had wrecked the car, which I then had repaired. Then he sold it or gambled it away. We really don't know what happened to it. Buying him a car, making all those trips to and paying a lot of money to STRAIGHT obviously was enabling and not helping at all. We thought we were doing right but we were enabling. When you are desperate, you will reach out to anyone who offers hope. We'd reached out to people and a program and not God. Reaching out to God is the only way for an addict to be healed. We unknowingly enabled instead of helped.

At the age of thirty-four years, while he was incarcerated in Virginia, a judge released him to a minister friend of mine who operated a Christian long-term drug rehab ministry. He was there for eighteen months, doing wonderful and close to graduating the Bible based program. He was enrolled at North Greenville University, making good grades and employed there as a chef in the university cafeteria. My wife and I drove 210 miles each day for over half the semester, transporting him back and forth from the university to the drug rehab facility. During this time, my uncle passed away and my cousin graciously allowed me to fix up his house so my son could live there rent free! Early one morning, the Lord woke me and said, *"Go check on your son."* I went to my uncle's house and the front door was standing open and there were empty beer cans on the floor. I was devastated. Two weeks later we found him in a disgustingly filthy drug house. He had lost over thirty pounds! We had bought him a nice used SUV and it was nowhere to be found. We never located the SUV.

I thought I was doing the right thing, helping him to become sober and be a productive citizen. I did so many wrong things trying to help instead of turning him over to God completely, I tried to help God when He didn't need my help. I got my son out of jail and released to my friend. I spent hours fixing up my uncle's house so he would have a nice place to live. His stepmother and I drove 210 miles a day for weeks so he could get a college education and better himself.

All of that mattered more to me than it mattered to him, because one fateful day, he left it all and went back to using drugs. All we did, fixing up my uncle's house, driving 210 miles per day, getting him out of jail and into a Christian, Bible based drug rehab program was for naught because I'd wanted it more than he did. I'd enabled him. It seemed I was doing the right thing, but I didn't listen to God and my minister friend who told me not to interfere. I went ahead of God and took matters into my own hands. I was an enabler. In my zeal to "fix" my son, I suppose I thought I knew more than God. It is never a good idea to take matters into your hands and go ahead of God. God is the healer, not me.

Four years later, he found his mother dead from an overdose of drugs. This sent him reeling in a more dangerous downward spiral than ever before. In 2012, we brought him home (again) after his mother's death. We'd hoped to help him get a new start. Our rules were simple: no drugs, no alcohol, no tobacco, and no lies. During his stay with us, he stole my cameras and computer and pawned them. He stole jewelry from his stepmother and money from her purse and he repeatedly lied to us. This made it necessary for me to put him out of our home. I asked my wife to leave the house while I did this most unpleasant task, because I wasn't sure what his reaction would be. This was one of the most unpleasant duties I have ever had to do, but to not carry it out would be enabling him again and turning our home into a house of chaotic insanity again. Thankfully, his reaction was one of remorse and I told him I would carry him wherever he wanted to go within a reasonable distance. He made a phone call, and I took him to a sleezy apartment building where he met up with some druggy friends. I can still see him standing there with his two suitcases as I drove off from that run-down apartment building. The look on his face was one of hopelessness, and I suppose the look on my face was the same, for I desperately wanted to stop and take him back home with me.

The next six years saw the drug abuse and his physical health deteriorate dramatically. He called me one day from Charleston, South Carolina, where he was living and asked me if I would come and get him because he needed help. He'd had several surgeries and been in the hospital many times since his mother's death. When I got to Charleston to pick him up, he was in a nasty, run-down motel. As I got out of my truck, I spotted someone carrying a man on his back. As I got closer, I saw it was my son being carried by one of his druggie friends and they both were high. I looked down at the sidewalk and saw a trail of blood on the concrete. This druggy friend had carried him from the pool to the motel door and his feet were dragging on the concrete. He suffered from drop foot and neuropathy, so he had no feeling in his feet and didn't realize that his toes on both feet were being dragged on the sidewalk. I just about lost it because his toes looked like raw hamburger meat. As I inspected their room, it was filthy with clothes, dirt, and pills all over the floor. Had I not been a follower of Jesus Christ, I fear I would have become violent. I learned that he and his friend had used meth earlier in the day. I left most of his stuff on the floor of the motel and drove us to a hotel where we spent the night. That night was very eventful as my son was very paranoid. He woke me up all during the night telling me that people were in the room and they were going to hurt him. The look on his face told me that he indeed was scared for his life. What a sad state to be in all because of drugs. I think I would have been better off to have driven the four hours home without any sleep than to have endured the night we spent. It really was a scary night. although he had never tried to harm me. I suppose I should have been more careful.

The next three months I worked to get him into a nursing home or an assisted living facility. He was in and out of the hospital and as a result we would lose his nursing home room. We finally found an assisted living facility that would take him and administer the daily IV antibiotic that he required. The day we were moving him into this facility, he told me that he didn't feel well, and a nurse took his temperature and told me to get him to the ER as soon as possible.

He was admitted to the hospital with endocarditis and MRSA. On September 20, 2018, the doctors told me that his immune system had shut down and the antibiotics were not working and there was nothing else they could do. On September 23, 2018, he was transferred to a hospice house where he died on October 1, 2018.

He was a handsome and intelligent young man who'd made the fatal mistake of taking that first drink. That drink led to a miserable life filled with mistakes, sickness, heartaches, and disappointments. It was a life that gave us only a glimpse of what he could have been. His addiction robbed him of the blessed life he could have had as a follower of Jesus Christ. Before he died, he told me that he had four other druggy friends that he hung out with as a teenager, and he was the only one still alive. Drugs rob, steal, and kill.

He told me that he knew God had called him to preach the gospel. He desperately wanted to help others who suffered from drug addiction. He wanted to write a book, and in fact had started the book. The title was, *Be Careful Who You Lie To, Especially Yourself, You May Just Start To Believe Them.* His introduction went like this, "The story of a man's life who believed in God and was baptized at an early age then walked down the road to hell for 35 years." There was a problem though, the years of drug abuse had robbed him of the ability to concentrate and focus. He would try, but his focus always went in another direction. He no longer had the ability to pull his thoughts together. He was no more than a prisoner locked in a dark dungeon of his own making, virtually useless for the kingdom of God. Drugs gave him the false sense of security that you can function normally while using. That is a lie straight from the pit of hell.

Some Characteristics of Addicts

A ddicts are selfish, self-seeking, and arrogant. They think only of themselves and their addiction.

Addicts are liars. They lie to protect their addiction. The life of the addict is all based on dishonesty and they can be very convincing. Even when you know they are lying, you will doubt yourself. The truth is not in them.

Addicts do not have listening ears. They are closed to the truth. The truth is opposite to who they are. They are constantly thinking about how they will get the next drink or fix. They are not interested in anything you have to say.

Addicts think that no one knows they are substance abusers. They have bought the lie. They think people are idiots. Most people will not call a drug addict on the carpet. They will just play along with them so as not to "hurt their feelings."

Addicts play the blame game. They will blame anyone or any circumstance for their plight. They become good at making up a reason to blame someone or something else. "It's not my fault."

Addicts think they are entitled. Sadly, friends, family, and "free programs" create a lot of this. Well-meaning people give to the addict because they feel sorry for them and this humanitarian act fuels entitlement in the addict's mind.

Addicts live in squalor. They do not practice personal hygiene and they do not clean up their living space.

Addicts mostly experience highs and lows. They are usually on the mountain top or in the pit below.

Addicts are paranoid. Meth, cocaine, heroin, and some prescription drugs will cause a person to be paranoid.

Addicts are usually financially poor.

Addicts are manipulators. Watch out! Addicts are convincing and are not afraid to approach family, friends, and strangers with a sad story. They learn quickly how to manipulate others.

Addicts are takers while friends and family tend to be givers (enablers). The addict will take from you as long as you are willing to give to them. They will take your last dime. They don't care if you lose your marriage, family, house, car, or your job if they get what they want.

This list of characteristics is what I have personally observed. Not every addict shows these characteristics, and they exist in different degrees in different people. I do believe that if a person becomes a substance abuser and allows Satan to build a stronghold in their spirit, they will eventually take on all these characteristics. When a person gets to this level of addiction, it is extremely difficult for the stronghold to be broken. I will not say it is impossible but as we will discuss later, it is nearly impossible. It requires great faith, prayer, and fasting.

Family Roles

(Taken from the internet, written by The American Addiction Centers Editorial Staff. Updated November 4, 2019)

Substance abuse is a family problem that affects not only the user but the entire family as well. Family members must navigate and endure the chaotic world of addiction, ultimately adopting short-term coping strategies that can create unwanted lasting effects. The roles of those who become a part of the addict's world are listed below.

The Addict

People struggling with substance abuse live in a constant state of chaos. Drugs become their primary way to cope with problems and feelings. He or she will stop at nothing to supply this need. As a result they burn bridges, lie, and manipulate those around them. They isolate themselves and angrily blame others for their problems. Adult addicts often must be treated like children because they are unable to function at their job or as parents, a spouse, and a caring, responsible neighbor. Within their family the addict's struggle creates a very difficult task for the entire family, yet the addict is only focused on the next drink or that next fix. The world revolves around them, causing the addict to become the center of attention. Other family members then unconsciously take on the rest of their enabling roles, trying vainly to provide "balance" to the family already thrown into the chaos of addiction.

The Enabler (The Fixer)

They make all the other roles possible. They try and keep everyone happy and smooth things over in order to protect the family. They make excuses for the addict's behaviors and actions and convince themselves that substance abuse doesn't exist (they live in denial) and they *never* mention getting help. They will do without and allow other family members to do without to give to the addict. There are often multiple enablers in a family. In many instances, they buy the lie of Satan that addiction is a disease, an incurable disease. This role is most often played by a spouse, but it may be taken on by the eldest child. The enabler is often put into "no win" situations by their commitment to support the addict. Without realizing the damage they are doing by assuming responsibility for fixing the family, they become so busy "fixing" the family that they don't realize the harm they are doing to everyone within the addict's life circle by enabling the addiction.

The Hero

Perhaps you're a Type A personality, a hardworking, over-achieving perfectionist, the hero who tries to bring the family together and create a sense of normalcy through his or her achievements. This role is usually taken on by the eldest child as they seek to give hope to the rest of the family. This need to do everything right tends to put an extreme amount of pres-sure on the hero, leaving them susceptible to stress related illnesses in later life.

The Scapegoat

The scapegoat becomes a safety valve for the family and often acts out in front of others (sometimes violently). They get blamed for the whole family's problems. They will rebel and make noise, anything to divert attention from the addict. They draw attention away from the addict in order to shield them from blame and resentment.

The Mascot

The family clown is always trying to deflect the stress of the dysfunctional family by supplying humor (sometimes cruel, harmful humor). This role is usually taken on by the youngest child; they are fragile, vulnerable, and desperate for the approval of others. They provide comic relief as a defense against pain and fear. Mascots often grow up to self-medicate with alcohol and drugs, thus perpetuating the cycle of addiction within the family.

The Lost Child

This role is usually taken on by the middle or the youngest child. They are shy, withdrawn, and sometimes thought of as "invisible" to the rest of the family. They don't seek or get a lot of attention from the rest of the family's members. These lost children will put off making decisions, and they have trouble forming intimate relationships. They choose to spend time alone as a way to cope. They are careful not to make problems, and they avoid any conversation about the "addicted family."

Some Types of Addictions

Tobacco	Food
Alcohol	Cell Phones, Computers, Social Media
Prescription Drugs	Gambling
Illegal Drugs	Vaping
Pornography	Self/Promoting Self
Sex	Work
Pedophilia	Hobbies
Homosexual Lifestyle	Sports

Consequences of Drunkenness

What Does God's Word Say?
(taken from the NKJV)

Wine is a mocker, strong drink is a brawler, and whoever is led astray by it is not wise.
(Prov. 20:1)

A *Mocker* is one who makes fun of, ridicules, or mimics others. A *Brawler* is one who will fight and is quarrelsome.

I have a friend who was an alcoholic and he told me that when he drank beer he got loud and was very funny and laughed a lot, just generally obnoxious. But when he drank liquor, he would pick a fight with anyone in the bar (and he was not a big man).

> Who has woe? Who has sorrow? Who has contentions? Who has wounds without cause? Who has redness of eyes? Those who linger long at the wine when it is red. When it sparkles in the cup. When it swirls around smoothly; at last, it bites like a serpent, and stings like a viper. Your eyes will see strange things and your heart will utter perverse things. Yes, you will be like one who lies down in the midst of the

sea, or like the one who lies at the top of the mast, saying: "They struck me, but I was not hurt; they have beaten me, but I did not feel it. When shall I awake, that I may have another drink." (Prov.23:29–35)

Solomon begins by asking five questions. He then gives an answer and a consequence to each of the questions.

I had a friend who was a homeless, street cocaine addict. He told me that a friend of his had gotten beaten up while he was drunk. The beating was so bad that one of his eyeballs was knocked out of its socket. When he awoke, the first thing he said was, "I need a drink."

It is not for kings O Lemuel, it is not for kings to drink wine, nor for princes intoxicating drink; lest they drink and forget the law, and pervert justice of all the afflicted. Give strong drink to him who is perishing, and wine to those who are bitter of heart. Let him drink and forget his poverty and remember his misery no more. (Prov. 31:4–7)

Kings cannot make wise decisions when they are drunk.

On the seventh day when the heart of the king was merry with wine, he commanded Mehuman, Biztha, Jarbona, Bigtha, Abagtha, Zethar, and Carcus, seven eunuchs who served in the presence of King Ahasuerus, to bring

Queen Vasti before the king wearing her royal crown, in order to show her beauty to the people and the officials for she was beautiful to behold. But Queen Vasti refused to come at the king's command brought by his eunuchs; therefore, the king was furious, and his anger burned within him. (Esther 1:10–11)

The king gave a rash command while he was drunk, one that cost the queen her position, because she refused to obey the king. It was against Persian custom for a woman to appear before a public gathering of men. It has been suggested by some historians that Queen Vasti was pregnant at this time and did not want to parade in front of a gathering of men. Whatever the reason, the queen and the king were both placed in a precarious situation because of the command Ahasuerus gave while he was drunk.

"And do not be drunk with wine, in which is dissipation; but be filled with the Spirit" (Eph. 5:18).

Dissipation means to be wasteful and extravagant, which leads to poverty.

But the fruit of the Spirit is love, joy, peace, longsuffering, kindness, goodness, faithfulness, gentleness, self-control.

Against such there is no law. (Galatians 5:22–23)

Now the sons of Noah who went out of the ark were Shem, Ham, and Japheth. And Ham was the father of Canaan. These were the sons of Noah and from these, the whole earth was populated.

And Noah began to be a farmer, and he planted a vineyard. Then he drank of the wine and was drunk and became uncovered in his tent. And Ham, the father of Canaan, saw the nakedness of his father, and told his two brothers outside. But Shem and Japheth took a garment, laid it on their shoulders, and went backward and covered their father's nakedness. So, Noah awoke from his wine, and knew what his younger son had done to him. Then he said: "Cursed be Canaan, a servant of servants he shall be to his brethren." And he said: "Blessed be the Lord, the God of Shem and may Canaan be his servant. May God enlarge Japheth, and may he dwell in the tents of Shem; and may Canaan be his servant." Noah got drunk, a poor example of a Godly man. (Gen. 9:18–27)

"The older women, likewise, that they may be reverent in behavior, not slanderers not given to much wine, teachers of good things" (Titus 2:3).

Woe to those who rise early in the morning, that they may follow intoxicating drink, who continue until night, till wine inflames them! The harp and the strings, the tambourine and flute, and wine are in their feasts; but they do not regard the work of the Lord, nor consider the operation of his hands. Therefore, my people have gone into captivity, because they have no knowledge; their honorable men are famished, and their multitude dried up with thirst. Therefore, Sheol has enlarged itself and opened up its mouth beyond measure; their glory and multitude and their pomp, and he who is jubilant, shall descend into it. People shall be brought down, each man shall be humbled, and the eyes of the lofty shall be humbled. (Isa. 5:11–15)

Isaiah was calling the nation of Judah back to God. They were drinking and partying and they had left God out of their lives, which allowed sin to come in. Both the honorable and the common men would die of hunger and thirst. Could this be America today?

When an unclean spirit goes out of a man, he goes through dry places seeking rest, and finds none. Then he says, "I will return to my house from which I came." And when he finds it empty and swept and put in order, then he goes and takes with him seven other spirits more wicked than himself, and they enter and dwell there; and the last state of the man is worse than the first. So shall it be with this wicked generation. (Matt. 12:43–45)

This verse explains why addicted people who have stopped using drugs, perhaps for years, and start using again find themselves in worse shape than they were in to begin with. When a person gets clean of drugs, they must come to the saving power of Jesus Christ. They must replace the emptiness with the Holy Spirit. Coming to Jesus through the power of the Holy Spirit is the only way. Without Him, there is no power over addiction. Only Jesus has power over addiction.

I had two good friends who were addicted to drugs and had been clean for many years only to start using again. They both were dead in less than six months after they began using. Drug addiction will kill you! It is nothing to play around with.

Unfulfilled and complacent people are easy targets for Satan.

Unguarded strength becomes your greatest weakness.

Be Careful Who You Hang
Around With
Choose Your Friends Wisely

*Blessed is the man who walks not in the counsel
of the ungodly, nor stands in the path of sinners,
nor sits in the seat of the scornful.* (Ps. 1:1)

've spent thirty-six years in the public school system as a teacher, coach, and principal. During that time, I've observed unsuspecting students as they chose to hang around students who would lead them down the wrong path. At first, I would see them walking with them at class change, then I'd notice them when they would stand and talk with the wrong crowd at lunch, before and after school, then they would be sitting with them at lunch and other school activities. This is a downward progression walking, standing, and sitting. Suddenly, these unsuspecting students have become one of them, the wrong crowd. It is so very important to choose your friends wisely, for they can elevate you to a closer walk with God or they can take you down to their level of ungodliness.

This is one principle that I could not get my son to understand. He would always contact and hang around his old druggy friends who would pull him down. He always had their phone numbers and knew how to get in contact with them. There is also a downward progression with these people—ungodly, sinful, scornful people.

The diagram below may help you to better understand this deadly downward progression.

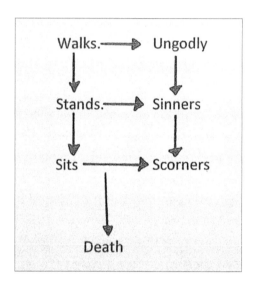

My son, if sinners entice you, do not consent if they say, come with us, let us lie in wait to shed blood, let us lurk secretly for the innocent without cause, let us swallow them alive like sheol and whole like those who go down to the pit. We shall find all kinds of precious possessions, we shall fill our houses with spoil; cast in your lot among us, let us all have one purse! My son, do not walk in the way with them, keep your foot from their path. For their feet run to evil, and they make haste to shed blood. Surely in vain, the net is spread in the sight of any bird, but they lie in wait for their own blood, they lurk secretly for their own lives. So are the ways of everyone who is greedy for gain; it takes away the life of its owners. (Prov. 1:10–19)

This sounds like modern day gangs within a socialistic society. Satan has blinded their eyes to the truth. They are unable to see that they are spreading the net for their own blood.

> Do not mix with winebibbers, or gluttonous eaters of meat; for the drunkard and the glutton will come to poverty, and drowsiness will clothe a man with rags. (Prov. 23:20–21)

> The righteous should choose his friends carefully, for the way of the wicked leads them astray. (Prov. 12:20)

My son could never break away from drug dealers, druggie friends, and wicked people. He told me that drug dealers and ungodly people would approach *him* to buy drugs and hang out. I told him that I had never been approached to buy drugs and that there were three things that led to this:

1. The way you dress.
2. The way you talk.
3. The way you act/behave.

> *Go from the presence of a fool.* (Prov. 14:7)

How Do You Recognize a Fool?

A fool's wrath is known at once. (Prov. 12:16)

A sk God to give you discernment, then just quietly watch and listen. It will not take long to recognize the fool.

> *As a dog returns to his own vomit, so a fool repeats his folly.* (Prov. 26:11)

As disgusting as it is, a dog will return to his vomit and eat it. A fool will also repeat his folly. You just need to watch and observe. My mother, the daughter of a poor sharecropper, told me that in the fall after the cotton was picked and sold that her father would take the money and binge drink until it all was gone. This occurred almost every year, leaving his family penniless as they faced the winter. This is not the behavior of a loving father but of an addict doing what addicts do. How sad.

> If a wise man contends with a foolish man, whether the fool rages or laughs, there is no peace. (Prov. 29:9)

You cannot convince a fool to be rational, and you cannot reason with a person who is drunk or high on drugs. If you try to convince a fool, then you have two fools arguing. Don't waste your time!

> Do not be envious of evil men, nor desire to be with them; for their heart devises violence, and their lips talk of troublemaking. (Prov. 24:1–2)

It is not difficult to recognize an evil person. Flee from their presence and do not desire what they possess.

> Do not be deceived, evil company corrupts good habits. (1 Cor. 15:33)

You will most definitely take on the characteristics of those you choose to hang around with. You will become like them. Satan is the great deceiver. Do not allow him to dupe you.

Make Sure Your Decisions Are God's Will for Your Life

"The way of the fool is right in his own eyes, but he who heeds counsel is wise" (Prov. 12:15).

I f you have doubts, seek wise counsel. Ask God to give you discernment to know right from wrong. He will answer your prayer. Pray and wait.

"There is a way that seems right to a man, but its end is the way of death" (Prov. 14:12).

"There is a way that seems right to a man, but its end is the way of death" (Prov. 16:25).

Why do you think Proverbs 14:12 and Proverbs 16:25 (the same verse) is in the Bible twice? You think maybe God thinks it is important?

It is sometimes easy to convince yourself that it is all right to do what everyone else is doing. You say, "Just this one time won't hurt." It only took one drink for my son to become hooked. Don't fall for Satan's lie. Do not allow Satan to deceive you as Eve was deceived in the garden,

"Do not enter the path of the wicked, and do not walk in the way of evil, avoid it, do not travel on it; turn away from it and pass on" (Prov. 4:14–17).

Turn from evil, flee, run, get away. Don't give Satan a foothold. Get away from evil, wicked people as quickly as possible. You should not be there in the first place. It is a choice that you make. Make the right choice.

Choices

M any times, the decisions we make deeply affect our lives years later. The decision to smoke the first cigarette, use the first illegal drug, take the first prescription pain pill, the first alcoholic drink, the first look at pornography, or engage in sex outside of marriage. All of these are choices, each of them is a decision that a person made by allowing Satan to convince them that "Just one time won't hurt, after all everyone else is doing it." At this juncture, they begin to question God's commands as Eve did in the garden. They are about to make a decision that will run counter to God's word. A decision that will lead to a life of loneliness, a life where the only thing that matters is the next drink or the next fix. Where they can't stay in the room with family because they must go out and smoke a cigarette. A life where they will do anything to get the drug. A decision that will lead to a broken marriage in which siblings turn against one another. Where parents lose control of the family unit and chaotic conditions arise as the family falls into bankruptcy. At this point, the family slowly crumbles into a state of disrepair because at one time a decision was made that seemed right, but its end was the way of death. They bought Satan's lie, they took the cheese, and the trap was sprung. The unsuspecting person who thought they were doing something that was harmless is now headed for the dreadful life of a drug addict.

When I was a middle school principal, I would have the "Get Smart Team" from the South Carolina Department of Corrections come and speak to our students each year. These are carefully screened inmates who talk to the students about making wise choices and the dangers of hanging around the wrong people and drugs and alcohol. In all the years I listened to them speak, I do not remember one who was not under the influence of drugs or alcohol when they committed their crime.

Choose Wisely! There is a way that seems right, but its end is the way of death. But there is also a way that is right, and that is the choice to follow Jesus Christ. By following Jesus lonely people who are imprisoned in their minds in chains in dark, dirty dungeons can experience the love and peace that only God can give.

Where fractured families that are disconnected from God and each other do not exist. Where generational sin and curses are broken. Christ died that we do not have to live in bondage, chained as prisoners in cold dark lonely dungeons of our own making—prisons of our own desires. Praise God that we do not have to endure such misery if we only humble ourselves and accept Him for what He did on the cross for our sins.

My son said to me before he died, "Dad, I did this to myself. Why did I not listen to you?" I suppose countless numbers of people have asked themselves that question "Why did I not listen and obey God's word?"

If you have not decided to follow Jesus Christ as your Savior and have not yet asked Him to come into your heart and save you from your sins, I urge you not to wait any longer. Romans

6:16 tells us that we are slaves to who we obey. Choose Jesus now or choose a life of sin and confusion, heartache, and guilt that will ultimately lead to a slow, painful death and hell.

John 3:16 tells us that God loves us so much that He sent his only begotten Son that whosoever believes in (trusts, clings to, relies upon) Him shall not perish (come to destruction, be lost) but have eternal (everlasting) life. If you haven't accepted Him, please don't wait any longer. You may not get a second chance. Are you willing to take that chance?

What Can Happen to a Family with a Member Who Suffers from Addiction

The goal of the family is to take care of the addict so the "good name" of the family is not tarnished. The family members take on the roles of codependency we discussed earlier. Each member spends their time in their own way going in their own direction to "fix" the addict. Inordinate amounts of physical and emotional energy are spent trying to fix this problem. All the while, much of the family's financial resources are used to "keep things quiet." Often, nothing is ever mentioned about the addiction or getting help. As the emotional and mental state of the family begins to wear thin, and the family's financial resources become depleted, the family is adversely affected as bills cannot be paid and other family members are prevented from doing and having things they would like because funds are being used so the addict can maintain his addiction. This places a hardship on the breadwinner(s) of the family. Frequently, the family will lose their home, cars are repossessed, jobs are lost, and the family becomes poverty stricken. Often, the parents divorce and the children are placed in foster care or sent to live with a family member, and older siblings and parents end up in volatile arguments the result in physical injuries, and emotional scars are worn for a lifetime.

While all of this is happening, the addict is only concerned with themself. Often, they do not participate in family gatherings and holiday events. Dishonesty, lies, and deception become the norm as the only thing that matters to the addict is where the next fix or drink is coming from.

My father had seven siblings and we had a lot of family gatherings at birthdays and holidays. All my aunts and uncles and my cousins would always be there, except for one uncle. I don't recollect him ever coming to a family event. Years later the family learned that he was addicted to gambling. I always wondered why he was always borrowing money from my dad, why he never owned a car, and why he still lived with my grandparents in the family homeplace. After my grandparents passed away, one of my other uncles found him in the homeplace dead from suicide. I now realize that all the signs of an addict were there, but I was young and didn't recognize them. I am pretty sure that he was not saved and is experiencing eternity in hell. This is a personal story of how a person can be a "closet addict." The signs are there if we will only look closely. People like this need the Lord, and they need someone to witness to them. If you have a family member, loved one, or acquaintance who you suspect has an addiction, look for the signs for they desperately need to hear the gospel. Will you be the one to take it to them?

Spiritual Warfare

I don't think a person just wakes up one day and decides that he/she wants to be a drug addict. Drug addiction is real, and it will kill you. When a person begins using drugs, it is a choice whether it is because of peer pressure, just to be sociable, or just curiosity. Whatever the reason, it opens the door that could lead to a life of misery, heartache, confusion, poverty, drug related illnesses, and finally death. It is usually a life lived without experiencing God's love and the joy one gets from knowing Him.

We must not forget that the battlefield is in the mind. Lies and deception are two of Satan's most used tools. These are the building blocks for a stronghold. Strongholds can cause a person to think in ways that block them from understanding God's word. Lies and false beliefs can only be dispelled with the truth. The more truth you bring into a situation, the more darkness must flee. Therefore, it is important to grow in God's word because it is the only offensive weapon listed in the spiritual armor in Ephesians 6. Satan can do nothing about your position in Christ, but if he can deceive you into believing his lies, then you will spend a lot of time questioning God's word and Satan will usually win the battle of doubt.

Paul writes in 2 Corinthians, "For though we walk in the flesh, we do not war according to the flesh. For the weapons of our warfare are not carnal but mighty in God for pulling down strongholds, casting down arguments and every high thing that exalts itself against the knowledge of God, bringing every thought captive to the obedience of Christ" (2 Cor.10:3–5).

Paul gives us the armor of God in Ephesians 6:

> Finally, my brethren, be strong in the Lord and in the power of His might. Put on the whole armor of God, that you may be able to stand against the wiles of the devil. For we do not wrestle against flesh and blood, but against principalities, against powers, against the rulers of the darkness of this age, against spiritual hosts of wickedness in the heavenly places. Therefore, take up the whole armor of God, that you may be able to withstand in the evil day, and having done all, to stand.
>
> Stand therefore, having girded your waist with truth, having put on the breastplate of righteousness, and having shod your feet with the preparation of the gospel of peace; above all, taking the shield of faith with which, you will be able to quench all the fiery darts of the wicked one. And take the helmet of salvation, and the sword of the Spirit, which is the word of God; praying always with all prayer and supplication

in the Spirit, being watchful to this end with all perseverance and supplication for all the saints and for me, that utterance may be given to me, that I may open my mouth boldly to make known the mystery of the gospel, for which I am an ambassador in chains; that in it I may speak boldly, as I ought to speak. (Ephesians 6:10–20)

We are commanded to stand and put on the whole armor of God, not part of it, to pray and to be watchful to the end. We are never told to "take a break," take off the armor, stretch, have a cup of coffee, stop praying and watching. This battle we are in is 24/7, therefore we must stay alert, stay in the word and never turn our backs on Satan. We are to stand and assume a battle-ready position. This is not playtime. It is not a dress rehearsal. This is the real thing and you had better be ready. Your mind had better be made up. You can rest assured that Satan and his demons want to keep you from hearing the truth; they want you to spend eternity with them in hell.

Strongholds exist all around us, but once a stronghold is established as a drug addiction, it is almost impossible to break it, no matter how innocently it began. As the stronghold becomes established in a person, the demons are not moved out easily. Just like a constrictor snake, that slowly squeezes its prey as it tries to break free, the constrictor never loses its grip on the helpless prey until it is dead. There is no way out. The choice to use drugs for the first time is a choice, after that? The victim is caught in that deadly downward spiral that leads to a slow suicide. Usually, it is a slow painful way to die that the family and the addict experience. One that ends in death from overdose, drug related illness, or suicide.

In Matthew 12, Jesus' disciples came to Him and asked, "Why could we not cast out the demon?" Jesus said, "This kind does not go out except by prayer and fasting" (Matt. 12:19–21).

I believe this demon had a stronghold on the boy, therefore it required more faith to cast it out. It takes a totally committed soul. There is no room for shallow commitment, no room for unbelief. These strongholds are so impenetrable that it takes a stronger faith in God to cast out "this kind" of demon.

In Matthew 17, Jesus' disciples asked him why they could not cast a demon out of a boy. Jesus answered and said, "Because of your unbelief (little faith, NIV). For assuredly, I say to you, if you have faith as a mustard seed, you will say to this mountain, move from here to there, and it will move; and nothing will be impossible for you. However, this kind does not go out except by prayer and fasting" (Matt. 17:14–21).

Mustard Seed Faith

The mustard seed was the smallest of seeds. Jesus was saying that if we have even a small amount of faith in Him, that is enough to move the mountains in our lives. I believe this also shows us what Jesus can do through a believer who had more faith than a mustard seed. If mountains in our lives can be moved with mustard seed faith, just think what can be done with faith the size of a date seed!

Prayer and Fasting

Jesus said in both these verses, "That kind" does not go out except by prayer and fasting. The question for every believer is, "Do you really believe in prayer and fasting?" Do you really believe Jesus' words? This is the question that every believer faces. If you are a believer, do you have even mustard seed faith? Do you have the discipline and faith to fast? If you are not a believer, would you come to Jesus now and ask Him to be your Savior and Lord of your life?

Do You Believe Demons Exist Today?

You must not forget nor question the fact that demons exist today and the strongholds they inhabit exist and are real. Many people believe that demons only existed in the Old and New Testaments and they do not exist today. In other words, they do not believe that spiritual warfare exists today. Just as they do not believe that demons exist today. They also believe they will not become addicted if they try drugs. They think they are invincible. They have bought the lie. Satan's greatest weapon is the lie and false reports.

As a believer, you dare not forget that Satan is a defeated foe. He has no hold on you or power over you except what you give him. Jesus paid your sin debt on Calvary that you do not have to be a slave to drugs. You do not have to be chained in a dark cell of your own making because of your addiction. You do not have to suffer a painful, empty, useless life, existing as a victim in your mind, a prisoner locked in a dungeon with no purpose in life, a life that you created for yourself. Your only hope is in Jesus Christ. He is the only way.

Jesus, because of His total commitment to and faith in His Father, has made a way out for you, a way that you do not have to suffer from an addiction. If you are a believer and can muster even as much faith as the size of a mustard seed, nothing will be impossible for you. You can move the mountains in your life. You do not have to fear Satan nor be prisoner to any addiction. Praise be to God!

Peter warns us in 1 Peter 5: "Be sober (not intoxicated, calm, able to think clearly), be vigilant (watchful, alert, on guard); because your adversary (your enemy) the devil walks about like a roaring lion, seeking whom he may devour (kill, consume, destroy)" (1 Peter 5:8).

Lions attack sick, young, or staggering animals; they choose victims who are weak, alone, or not alert. One example of this may be found on YouTube. "Battle at Kruger" shows a pride of lions attacking a young water buffalo. Watch as the lions are patient and take turns on their prey. Watch to the end as the lions go down to defeat. As the lions are defeated, so was Satan defeated by Jesus at Calvary.

Helps to Prevent Sin and Addiction

Choose Friends Wisely. Resist Being Part Of The "Group."

Never Put Yourself In A Situation Where You Have To Say No.

Choose Your Friends Wisely. Be Very Careful Who You Hang Around.

Never Smoke The First Cigarette Or Joint.

Never Vape.

Choose Friends Wisely. Be Careful With Whom You Associate.

Never Take The First Drink Of Alcohol.

Never Take The First Pain/Opiate Pill.

Choose Your Friends Wisely, It Could Mean Your Life.

Never Use The First Illegal Drug.

Never Take The First Look At Pornography.

Choose Friends Wisely. Check Them Out First.

Never Engage In Illicit Sex.

Never Take Counsel From A Fool, Non-Christian, Or A Person Willfully Living In Sin.

Choose Friends Wisely, Observe, Look, And Listen Before Approaching.

Never Take Off The Armor Of God.

Pray, Read God's Word, And Fast For Strength To Resist Satan's Temptations.

Never Listen To "Friends" Who Talk/Brag About The "Fun" They Have Engaging In Illicit, Sinful Activities. Turn Away From Them. Flee From Them.

Choose Friends Wisely.

Summary

T he best way to avoid drug addiction is to never begin using. Once a person begins, the door has been opened for a possible life of horror where pain and sorrow, poverty, sickness, and a separation from family and God and a slow death are the norm.

Make no mistake about it, drugs will kill you, just as they killed my son. It was a slow, painful death that was spread over a thirty-year period. It was a miserable existence filled with dishonesty and a lack of trust, one that caused family and friends to finger-point and question one another.

Then there are the "roller coaster rides" where the addict appears to be "cured" only to have everyone's hopes and dreams crushed as a time of sobriety is most always followed by a long period of substance abuse. The roller coaster ride is experienced often in the lives of the addict and their family. All of this because the addict made a conscious decision to try the drug just once. Doctors, psychologists, and worldly counselors tell us that drug addiction is a disease, an incurable disease. The Bible, however, tells us that it is a choice, a choice to follow Jesus Christ or a choice to follow sin and a worldly view where there is a contentious spiritual battle raging where strongholds exist, and where Satan is walking around like a roaring lion seeking whom he may devour. This is a battle that you will most assuredly lose without Jesus Christ. If drug addiction is an incurable disease as the world tells us, then why does it only affect people who have chosen to take the first drink, drug, or cigarette? People who never begin never have to worry about becoming addicted.

Don't Forget:

There Is A Way That Seems Right To A Man, But Its End Is The Way Of Death.

Be Careful Who You Listen To And What You Believe.

Do Not Buy Satan's Lie. Don't Take The Cheese And Spring The Trap That Could Possibly Lead To A Life Of Addiction.

A Hard Choice

P aul tells us in 1 Corinthians 6: "Your body is a temple of the Holy Spirit who is in you, whom you have from God, and you are not your own? For you were bought at a price, therefore glorify God in your body and in your spirit, which is God's" (1 Cor. 6:19–20).

We are commanded to glorify God in our body and spirit. Drug abuse is not glorifying God. God the Father made a way through His Son Jesus Christ that we do not have to be in bondage and become a slave to drugs. The choice is yours, choose Jesus and a life of freedom and joy in Him or choose drugs and friends who will lead you to these vices and a life of pain, suffering, and death. Life gives you two choices, regret the past or change the present. You can never go back, so make the change. Accept Jesus today. Life is not a dress rehearsal. It is your choice. Choose wisely or accept the painful death that will surely follow if you choose drugs and the way of the world. Before my son died, he said to me, "Daddy, why would I not listen to you? You warned me. I have no one to blame but myself."

Drug addiction is a hard way of life; therefore, it must be dealt with harshly. Whether family member or friend, you cannot afford to feel sympathetic toward the addict. You cannot give them money when they are broke because they used their money on drugs and worldly pleasures. You cannot let them remain in your home when they are using drugs and stealing from you. There comes a time when you have to say, "Enough, I am sick and tired of being sick and tired. This insanity must stop. I will no longer enable you to continue this insane way of life." This is hard to say and even harder to carry out. To put a loved one on the street in the winter is a difficult thing to do. The addict has made his/her choice, so the family or a member of the family must make a choice . . . a hard choice. Often, the hard choice is not made, and the insanity goes on and on, never stopping. The addict and the family coexist in anger and misery. Happiness is rarely experienced, while dishonesty and a lack of trust is dealt with daily.

ADDICTION WILL TAKE YOU WHERE YOU DON'T WANT TO GO,
KEEP YOU LONGER THAN YOU WANT TO STAY,
AND COST YOU MORE THAN YOU WANT TO PAY.

In these few pages, we have covered a lot of information regarding substance abuse and addiction.

We have established that the choice to use drugs is just that, a choice. And once the choice is made to try a drug, the door has been opened to a possible life of addiction.

We have shown that all of this is orchestrated by Satan and that the battlefield is in the mind and, just as Eve was deceived in the garden, Satan wishes to plant seeds of doubt and deception in your mind.

Neil T. Anderson in his book *The Bondage Breaker* writes:

> Christians who hold the extreme view that demons were active when Christ was on the earth, but their activity has subsided today, are simply not facing reality.

> God's people wrestling against dark spiritual forces is not a first century phenomenon, nor is it an option for the Christian today; it's unavoidable. The kingdom of darkness is intent on making your life miserable and keeping you from enjoying and exercising your inheritance in Christ. Your only options in the conflict are how and to what extent you're going to wage the battle.

> Satan's ultimate lie is that you are capable of being the god of your own life, and his ultimate bondage is getting you to live as though his lie is truth. Satan is out to usurp God's place in your life. And whenever you live independent of God, focusing on yourself instead of the cross, preferring material and temporal values to spiritual and eternal values, he has succeeded. The world's solution to this conflict of identity is to inflate the ego while denying God the opportunity to take His rightful place as Lord. Satan couldn't be more pleased—that was his plan from the beginning.

Two Considerations Are Important Here:

1. You must determine in your mind and spirit not to do drugs. You must know in your spirit that your answer will be "NO" if you are tempted. Daniel made up his mind beforehand that he would not defile himself with the king's delicacies and wine. He knew what his answer would be. "But Daniel purposed in his heart that he would not defile himself with the portion of the king's delicacies nor with the wine which he drank" (Daniel 1:8). He purposed in his heart. The only way you can purpose in your heart successfully is through Jesus Christ. If you seek to overcome self by self-effort, it is a hopeless struggle. You must follow Christ and be led by the Holy Spirit down the path of death to self. Paul wrote in 2 Corinthians 4: "We who live are constantly being delivered over to death for Jesus' sake, that the life of Jesus also may be manifested in our mortal flesh" (2 Cor. 4:11).

2. Do you really believe what you believe? Do you believe in the power of prayer? Do you believe that God is more powerful than Satan and his demons of hell? Do you believe that faith in Jesus Christ and being clothed with the whole armor of God will save you from the fiery darts of Satan? Do you believe that God the Father sent Jesus, His only Son to die on a cross so that you can spend eternity in heaven with him? Do you really believe this?

If you have doubts about this and haven't invited Jesus into your heart to save you from your sins, I invite you to do so today. He is the way, the only way. He is the Light of the World. He is Truth. Only He can save you from your sins! Only He can save you from a life of addiction. It is your choice. Choose Jesus Christ and choose eternal life or choose sin and choose eternity in hell. THE CHOICE IS YOURS.

The Following Pages
Contain Some of My Son's
Writings

The Roads of Life

Life is a journey not a destination
We travel many roads
We make many choices
Some good some bad
Some happy some sad

As we walk down the roads
Some narrow some wide
Sometimes we're weak
Sometimes we're strong

We often feel things and don't know why
At times we laugh and at times we cry

But my experience my friend
And it proves to be true
No matter what
God's there for you

Saved

I'm saved by grace, not of me
But the one I cannot see
By the one hung on a tree
Saved by grace eternally

I've run, I've hid, I've moved afar
I've drunk away my worries in the bars
Shot the dope, and smoked the crack
Satan's demons all over my back

I've cried, I've moaned
I've looked for answers on the phone
Pastors, doctors, lawyers too
They can't save me from this craze
Only Him by His grace

I want to tell you how I feel
About that day on Golgotha's hill
You took a beating, was slapped with chains
You died and rose but still your love remains
You love me now eternally because
You hung on that tree
Now may I finish this race
Because I'm saved by your grace

The Day Jesus Took Mama Away

I'll never forget the day Jesus took mama away
I walked in and found her lying that way
All cold and hard, yellow and blue
She looked so alone
Me without a clue

My heart started racing, my teeth began to chatter
I dropped to my knees
What's the matter?
I looked up above into the sky
Screamed out to God...No! Why, Why, Why?

The street was lit up with all kinds of people
Me, I just wanted to be under a steeple
I screamed and I cried, I didn't understand
Why such a bad thing could happen to man

They wheeled her off and I began to reason
Her soul would be with Jesus just in time for the season
No more pain, arguments, or tension
But instantly with God, PopPop, and David for Christmas

Not right then, but now I see why
I found you that day and had to say goodbye
I'll miss you forever, but I'll see you again
Your spirit is with me and you're still my best friend!
I Love You.

No More Fears

Walking alone on the city streets
Rain drenched my soul scared and confused
Alone and abused
Feeling like I want to die

All the pain I caused myself
My family and my friends
Built inside my stone-cold heart
Tears in my eyes

I looked to the sky and asked the Lord
Lord, please help me
He gave me the will
I saw the light
He took away my fear

Thank you, God, Oh thank you God
Because your Son died on the cross
I have no more fears
No more fears
No more tears of pain

Today I have a future,
I walk in the light of God
Joy fills my heart
Peace is what I strive for

God's Always There

On that day I started to cry
Life had no meaning, I wanted to die
As I looked in the mirror and looked to the sky
I screamed out to God Please tell me why?

Why all these feelings of misery and shame
Help me please life feels like a game
I'm tired of the hurt, can't stand the pain
Oh God please take me so peace I may gain

As the tears started flowing down my face to the ground
A warm gentle feeling came over me
Could it be peace I had found?

The obsession it left me, a smile came on my face
Suddenly, the world wasn't such a bad place
I felt God had replaced hate with His grace

Oh, for so long how I've hurt inside
I turned on God and replaced him with pride
But he never left me, on His back I did ride

Brother let me tell you like others told me
There's no freedom like it, for yourself you shall see

Now there is joy, there is peace, there is a smile on my face
I don't feel I'm in bondage and caught up in the race

God, I'm forever thankful for you spared my life
So that I may sense you
And have peace, have love, have joy, and not strife
Now for all these long days that you carried me
I'll humbly be here for whatever you need

Thank you, oh God!

I found these two prayers in my son's journal. They were written several months before he died in October 2018 while he was in a nursing home.

> Father, I have demonized my mind, emotions, and physical body. I need you more than ever. I'm so tired and stricken because of my sin but I will do my best to walk in your Holy Spirit. Please protect me from Satan as I learn to submit. I'm a worm in this fallen world. Please feed me the truth and heal my body from all these physical elements that Satan uses to try and bring me down. I prayed for health and over and over you have given it to me only to find out I've done it again. Take deceit, lying, and questioning you and heal my sin drenched body. Let the fruit of the Spirit just overwhelm me. Give me rest at night and wisdom to study. I want to know you like you know me, at least what I'm capable of knowing. I've been a fool, please replace that with a contrite heart. Oh God, I feel dirty, and grief stricken. Bring us— myself, and my parents—together. Be with me only to do righteous things, things of above. Foolishness stops and righteousness begins. I love my parents. Stop the little things as I see them. They continue to kill our relationship. Send me to get therapy that I may keep my mouth shut and learn from the elderly and only pray to you in the Spirit. Help me to stop

the little things because there are no little sins. They can and will corrupt and ruin my life. God, I pray from here on out that you give me the wisdom to NOT be deceitful. Help me to treat my parents with honor and respect and fill me with your Holy Spirit. Help me that I may have love, joy, peace, patience, kindness, gentleness, and self-discipline, the one I lack most. Help me to put you first, others second, and me last. Teach me from the inside out that I may not fear anything including death. I would love nothing more than to lie down each night knowing and believing that you are my Savior, King, and Lord and for my parents to do nothing more than to trust me. That I may treat them with honor and respect. That I will stop worrying about my health and know that you are all knowing and all powerful and you have a plan for me, but I must let the past go. That I shall greet my father daily with a hug and lift my stepmother's spirit by giving her encouragement and at the same time just love her. I've been a fool long enough. I pray for 100% total forgiveness. Now it's time to put it into action. Talk is cheap, actions speak so much louder than words. Take all anxiety, fear, and worrying away from me so I can worship you in Spirit and Truth.

Father, I pray that you will take this mountain of physical pain and cast out all demons and bind and loose them. I can't do this on my own, or even come close. I ask for forgiveness for my trickery and disobedience. You have gotten my attention with this foot and back. You have taken away the taste for crack cocaine and pain pills, and I don't know what to do with this mind, body, and soul I'm left with. I beg of you to get me through this. Please, oh God, hear my cry and heal my body. It's not pleasant but I won't fail if I keep my eyes on you and trust you with all my heart and not lean on my own understanding. Please keep chipping away until there are no more pills, no more deceitfulness, and lying. I'm so afraid of letting go of Clonipin because it takes away the fear, but you say, "Be anxious for nothing but by prayer and supplication in everything cast my fears upon you."

I'm so sorry of a person I keep struggling with what the world says are little things, or little lies, "Oh it was a small deceitful act. How could you not approve?" I'm nothing without Jesus. Please get Satan and his demons off me. Cast them out and give me a clean heart. Oh God make me clean inside and out. Heal me from head to toe. Let your will be done and help me climb this mountain. I just can't do it alone. Keep blessing me and don't let me die but let me continue to study and please pierce my heart and write your commands on the tablet of my heart. Teach me true love. Be with Mitchell and my dad and stepmom. Please reconcile our relationship that's always my fault. Keep my eyes on you and teach me how to live your way. I want to spend eternity with you, oh Lord. Please don't give up on me. Thanks for the assisted living facility and I pray you will keep my mouth shut, with no complaining and backbiting, just your word daily. I want you to be proud of me. As I write this, I am bombarded with negative and confusing thoughts. I bind and loose these thoughts. I need your help writing this book. I need obedience and concentration. I believe you have great plans in store for me and my relationship with you, my parents, and my family. Your word says if I follow your ways, I will reap great things. I believe you want great things for me. I believe you want the best for me. You've given me a great vision that I can live to be 86 if I stop poisoning my body. This immune deficiency and Hep C, you will heal me. You didn't bring me this far for no reason. I put you in the driver's seat. Keep me safe and give me wisdom and above all teach me how to love you with all my heart, all my soul, and all my mind. It's hard and I hate it, it's like I am programmed to be one way and I argue with myself and even try to deceive you. Please teach me not to make decisions that have negative consequences.

I want to go to church and Bible study with Daddy. All I must do is die daily. You have already healed me. I will truly be a new creation. Teach me love, agape love, the way you love me. No more relapses as the world calls it. It's plain old sin, sin, rotten nasty sin and I want nothing to do with it. Maybe you will bring me a good Christian woman one day and I can have a child or two. I praise you. That is one thing I never did, or your will didn't allow me to do is have a child because I wouldn't have taken care of it. I had my own plan to go to Charleston and your plan was just the opposite. You amaze me. I have no more chances. I must see doctors. I pray by your power that you will heal the Hep C and this drop foot. You already have 2000 years ago and by my faith I believe I'm healed. I'm willing to do whatever you put in my path. Jesus, oh how did you do it? Temptation, but you never gave in even though you were total man, total God, and total Spirit. Now you and your Spirit live inside of me. I pray that I follow your lead. I don't want to die young, and I don't have to. I just need to be obedient and have faith and in return I will receive eternal life. WOW! What will it be like? On one hand I'm apprehensive and scared, on the other hand, I'm excited. You know my thinking, forty years of sin in, sin out. Scared off my laurels about death. You have shown me time and again, you will never leave me or forsake me. Please bring Marianne and her family back to me. Right now, it's you and me. Please don't take your healing hands off me. Keep teaching me, chipping away, until one day I'm with you. I want to enter your kingdom because you are pleased with me. This medical stuff really has me baffled and scared. May I have a good night's sleep? Oh, how much I am wanting to get to you, using my daddy as a perfect daddy, but he admits to me when he sins.

Please don't give up on me now. When I need courage, you are there to encourage me. Oh, how I am like David, I'm after your heart. You have brought me so far, please, I pray, don't stop now. Please provide a safe environment for me to do rehab and give me wisdom to never complain, argue, or be backstabbing. The drugs are pretty much gone, but your love and teaching have never left as if it was yesterday. Teach me and show me how to walk the narrow path.

My son wrote this while he was staying in a hotel before he got into an assisted living facility several months before he died in October 2018.

I say I love Jesus and I want to love Jesus, but honestly, I've used that name in vain so much that I ask Father God to show me what love is.

He loved me so much that He came to earth and was crucified to relieve me from all the sin I choose to sit in. I let it go now. Take it God. I give it at the foot of the cross. Life has its struggles and that isn't just because of me. God created the world and every single person in it. It's my job to carry His message so others don't have to go through what I choose to go through. Death is one thing I can't control, so why would I keep going to human beings to heal me? Guess what? Nothing's changed—no pill, no speech, nothing will save us except God. All He asks of us is to believe and be obedient. God, you brought me through many snares of death and preserved me. All He wants is me and me totally. Oh, how I want this. Jesus said, "Let not your heart be troubled for in heaven there are many mansions, and I am going to live forever." I'm just passing through. It's a supernatural thing, it's not natural and God gives us just enough information because we couldn't handle it anyway. Jesus is my Savior. I've sinned so much, saying I repent only to turn and do it again. Lord, prayer is the key. Why do I have such a hard time with certain things? Deceitfulness, guilt, and shame have always driven me to dope and alcohol, because I cannot stop hanging around the wrong people and believing the lies of Satan to the point it has nearly killed me many times. I beg for your forgiveness because it's natural for me to just live the way I've been living for forty years. You spoke to me and said you will give me forty more years, but I must submit, take what I know is true and please keep stacking more and more of your grace on me. That's my desire. You have given me the opportunity to have my parents back. One mistake will blow it all. I have selfish reasons for this because I want that relationship. I see that I have hurt and disappointed them so many times. Yet my father comes here every day to give me my medicine because I'm so sin sick, I can't even manage my own money and medication.

Reveal to me what you need from me daily. I must die to self—daily. Nine times out of nine what I think is right because it feels right is nothing but lies. Drunkenness and sorcery are nothing but sin. If I continue to practice that, you can't use me, and the consequences are great that it will be death. I'm not ready to meet you face to face yet. I must grow, serve, love, and be honest.

May I be a child to my stepmom? She always wanted that and what did I do? I rebelled because of all kinds of reasons. I even tried to bargain with you and make light of a sin like dipping. It says right on the can its deadly, but that's not enough. I need it because of blah,

blah, blah. You are an all-knowing God and how dare I barter with you. Please, one last time, forgive my past and raise me up to be a mighty servant for you. This is a shell my soul and spirit are in for a time. It's time to make my choice of what to do about eternity. I know you exist in my heart, in my soul, and in my spirit.

It took Moses forty years of walking in circles being miserable until God choose to speak to him through an old bush. I need not try and find a bush because you have shown me your existence in visions. You allowed the devil to show me that he also exists. It's real. Eternity is real and I'm choosing to walk the narrow path. That situation today showed me exactly how every step I take, I must be on guard because just when I'm not, Satan knows and puts temptation right in my face. Praise God, that guy ran and disappeared. I felt and saw your presence. I had no reason to take the nasty roach, which is straight from hell. I should have flushed it and been done, but no, I had to do it my way, like I deserve something for that roach. Before, the old man would have raised almighty hell until I got my way. Like I deserve a free night. These people have been so nice to me, but the weak flesh rises. I do it my way and Satan set it up, he set me up for failure. Glory be to God. I give you, my praise. I submit to you. Resist the devil and he will flee. I can't get enough of your word; I desire to get and stay in your will. You have great things ahead for me. Why fear death? You promised eternity in heaven to me, and I promise things to you daily and fail miserably. That's how rotten my flesh is. Thank you, praise you, that situation could have been devastating, but you rescued me.

And more is coming. I beg of you to heal this disease-ridden body that I may be an obedient servant and stop straddling the fence. I talked to my stepmom today, she's a blessing. I never want to hurt her again. She doesn't deserve anything but love from me. When we spend time together going shopping, I want to ask her to be my mother, something I should have done many years ago.

As you can see, my son desperately wanted healing from his addiction. I have seen him on his knees crying out to God to heal him of his addiction. The fatal mistake he made was taking that first drink at twelve years of age.

You notice in his writings that he realized his condition was due to self- inflicted drug abuse. The statement he made in his poem "No More Fears" about being "all alone" and his "stone cold heart" sends chills up my spine each time I read it. Satan wants you to feel alone and heartless, callous, insensitive, and in-human. Satan wants to control you and when the addict feels this way, they will turn to drugs to escape reality. What a pitiful existence.

My brother-in-law was an alcoholic. At one point he was drinking a quart of vodka per day. His doctor was preparing to place him on the liver transplant list and told him he had 90-120 days to live. He told me that he humbled himself, got on his knees, asked Jesus to come into his heart and save him from his sins and to heal him from his addiction to alcohol. From that day on, he has not had a drink of alcohol and that was 15 years ago. He told me that God healed him and he doesn't have any desire to drink. He is a happy retired man who praises God daily for his sobriety and another day to live for Christ.

If you are struggling with an addiction I urge you to humble yourself, bring it to the cross, ask Jesus to be your Savior and forgive you of your sins and free you from your addiction. Jesus died a terrible death on the cross that you do not have to suffer from addiction. Claim it and be healed. Praise God that He loved us enough to give up His only Son that we might live a life free of addiction.

Photo Gallery

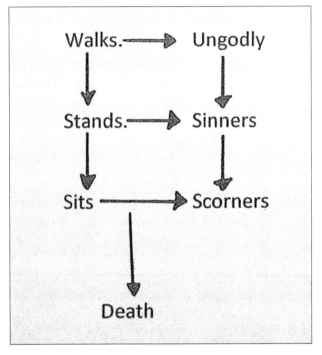

Diagram showing the downward spiral of sin in Psalm 1 (P.15)

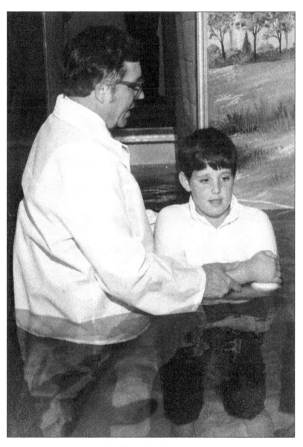

Andy baptized at age 9

Andy's Re-baptism at age 36

Andy and his step-mom

Andy and me

Andy and me

Andy and his grandmother

Andy giving his testimony at his graduation from
"Home with a Heart", a drug rehab program.

David Andrew Sloan

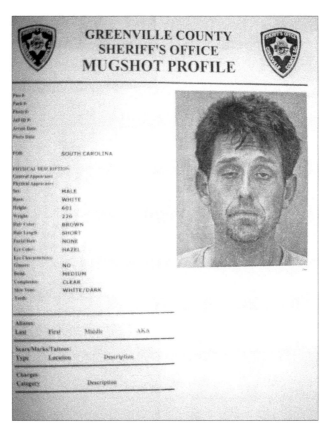

Mugshot after one of his arrests.

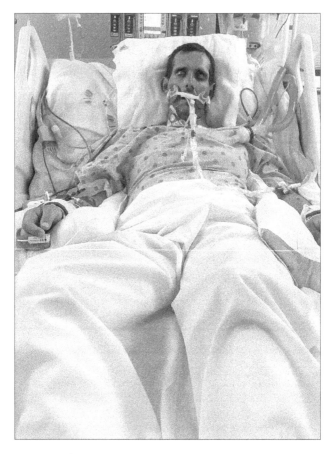

Andy in ICU at MUSC due to a drug overdose.

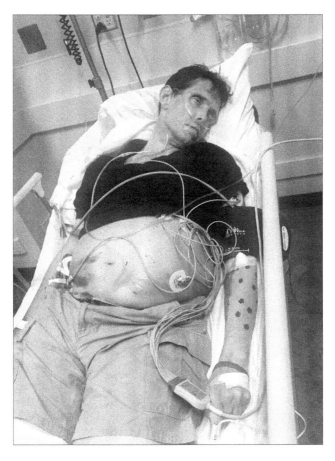

Andy in the ER just several weeks prior to his death.
His body had stopped responding to antibiotics

CPSIA information can be obtained
at www.ICGtesting.com
Printed in the USA
BVHW090408160222
629082BV00012B/1076

9 781662 839474